For Sale By Owner 30 Day Success Formula

By **Mitchell Hell** and **Matthew Hell**

EauClaireHomeBuyers.com

LIMIT OF LIABILITY/ DISCLAIMER OF WARRANTY:
THE INFORMATION PROVIDED IN THIS PUBLICATION IS
DESIGNED FOR INFORMATIVE PURPOSES ONLY IN REGUARD
TO THE SUBJECT MATERIAL COVERED. EVERY EFFORT HAS
BEEN MADE TO THE ACCURATCY OF THE CONTENT OF THIS
PUBLICATION AND SHALL NOT LIABLE FOR ANY LOSSES,
CLAIMS OR DEMANDS IN RELATION TO THIS PUBLICATION
THOUGHOUT THIS ENTIRE PUBLICATION FROM THE
FORMATION OF THE EARTH TILL THE END OF TIME. THIS
PUBLICATION IS SOLD WITH THE UNDERSTANDING THAT THE
AUTHORS OR PUBLISHERS ARE NOT ENGAGED IN
ACCOUNTING, RENDERING ANY LEGAL SERVICES OR ADVICE.
IF LEGAL ASSISTANCE OR OTHER PROFESSIONAL ADVICE IS
REQUIRED, THE PROFESSIONAL SERVICES OF A
PROFESSIONAL PERSON SHOULD BE CONTACTED. ALL
EFFORTS HAVE BEEN MADE TO AID YOU IN SELLING YOUR
HOUSE QUICKLY. ALTHROUGH WE CANNOT CONTROL
MARKET CONDITIONS OR OTHER FACTORS THAT
CONTRIBUTE TO SELLING YOUR HOUSE, THE AUTHORS AND
PUBLISHER TAKE NO RESPONSIBILITY HOW QUICK YOUR
HOUSE SELLS.

DEDICATION

This book is dedicated to all of our clients and our city. If it wasn't for you telling us your needs, we would never have created this book for you and would be able to share our selling program! Thank you for choosing us to guide you sell your house! We have left no stone unturned and are only giving you proven strategies to sell your house on your own using the strategies we use in our business when we buy and sell numerous houses every month

Table Of Contents

Preface iv

CHAPTER 1

LET ME GUESS… 1

CHAPTER 2

Which Selling Strategy is Right for You? 5

CHAPTER 3

Types of Buyers 8

CHAPTER 4

Get the Price Right! 10

CHAPTER 5

Staging the House for Sale 13

CHAPTER 6

Be Ready To Receive Buyer Phone Calls 17

CHAPTER 7

Marketing Your House for Sale 24

CHAPTER 8

Pre-screen Potential Buyers 39

CHAPTER 9

Meet With Buyer and Show Your House 42

CHAPTER 10

Schedule Closing With an Attorney   45

CHAPTER 11

Consider A Real Estate Investor   46

Final Word   49

30 Day Success Formula Checklist   50

Eau Claire Home Buyers

Preface

What you will learn in the FSBO 30 Day Success Formula:

✓ Our **7 Step 30 Day Success Formula** To Sell Any House In 30 Days or Less.

✓ Simple mind tricks to make sure you **always get top dollar** for your house. This alone was worth $5,519.

✓ **4 Proven Marketing Techniques** to attract numerous potential buyers to your house-Just copy our messages and let the buyers roll in.

✓ How to make sure you ONLY talk to buyers who can pay for your house NOT tire-kickers.

✓ How to use the internet and websites to reach **hundreds of potential buyers**-if you're not a computer person, don't worry, we take you step by step and make it easy.

✓ Why you **should not** put a "For Sale By Owner" sign in your yard-we tell you sign you should use.

✓ The #1 place on Facebook to **find potential buyers instantly.**

✓ **And much much more…**

Note from Mitch Hell:

<u>Welcome and congratulations</u> for investing in this book that will show you a proven step by step formula to sell your house on your own as quickly as possible in todays market! We are happy you are here and excited to see your results!

Mitch Hell
EauClaireHomeBuyers.com
FSBO 30 Day Success Formula

CHAPTER 1

LET ME GUESS...

If I may, I would like to guess that you are in the market to sell your house. Am I correct? You are a do-it-yourselfer and you have heard that selling your own house saves you ton of money and time.

If that is the case, I am proud of you! You are a person that takes charge of their situation and is looking to get results! That attitude, is what you need to sell your house quickly!

Nowadays, people are busy and that is often the reason why homeowners list their house with a Real Estate Agent. But, as it appears, it takes a while for a Real Estate Agent to sell houses in today's market.

Why do you think this is?

There are two main reasons for this including, but not limited to, the following;

1.) The Agent has many other houses to sell besides yours. Due to the overwhelming number of homeowners wanting to sell a house, real estate agents cannot focus solely on your house. This isn't the fault of the agent, but the result of the business they are in. Most homeowners sell their house through a real estate agent so their plates are pretty full. What usually happens is the agent will list your house on the MLS and put their sign in your yard. Then they let other buyers know about your house for sale. They then usually wait for a buyer to show interest or another agent to show interest because the other agent may have a buyer looking for that type of house. It often takes some time before the house sells.

2.) The Agent has the same marketing as other agents. When you look at a house that is listed with a real estate agent, usually you can assume that the sign will say the same thing. It will mention that it is for sale and it will show a logo of the real estate agency and it will list a number to call. Each agencies signs differ but they all say the same thing. This makes it hard for any one sign to stand out. Most agents don't aggressively market your house for sale because they don't have time or the budget to market each house they have listed because again, as I have said, they have a lot of houses under contract to sell.

Since you are a do-it-yourself, you have options at hand. You will be in charge of everything, from start to finish when selling your house. How quickly you sell your house is going to be determined by you.

This may cause a little anxiety though…right? All of a sudden, all the weight is on your shoulders…

Some homeowners are a little timid when it comes to selling their own house because they don't know how to go about doing it. The questions of paperwork, how to market your house for sale, how to talk to buyers, all come to mind and this can prevent a homeowner to take charge and do it themselves.

You may be feeling some of the same feelings and that is completely normal.

By selling your own house, you will also be saving a lot of money. Real Estate Agents usually charge a commission of about 3-6% of the houses selling price. For example, if your house sold for $100,000.00, you may be charged $3-6,000.00. Most homeowners will pay this amount because the agent does everything for them and it is sometimes easier that way. For some homeowners that need to sell, that is what is best for them, but for some, (You, Me, and other homeowners that call our office) it's something we would like to undertake and reap the benefits.

What we say is why pay someone to do something you can do yourself but, only when you know how to properly do it? And you will be keeping that money in your pocket! In our opinion, that is a better deal!

We will be showing you exactly how we at Eau Claire Home Buyers sell our houses we have in our inventory. We don't like to hang on to houses for very long as our paycheck is tied to being able to sell the house, so we needed to become very proficient at selling houses every month.

We have many unconventional methods to sell a house quickly as people have said, so be ready and open minded for it! We teach the unconventional ways to sell houses and that's what makes us so different from a standard real estate agent. And when you sell your house differently, you get attention and that is the whole point of this program.

Getting your house the attention it deserves and in turn that will drive a ton of eye balls and prospective buyers to your house!

A common problem for sellers is that they don't get buyers looking at their house or buyers calling them. All this means is their marketing is subpar. They must be doing something that either doesn't work or they are not doing enough marketing.

But, you don't have to worry about having that challenge anymore! This program will expose you to the best ways to let the world know your house is for sale. This program is a **marketing method** because selling your house quickly is much easier when you have tons of people looking at your house.

This program is also, **a system, that will make your life a lot easier**. What a "system" is is a process that will connect the dots of selling a house and make it as streamline as possible. A system is your key to successfully selling your house and we show you how we do it in our business of buying and selling houses and how you can copy it!

With all this said, the systems and marketing methods in this program will have you knowing more than 99% of your competition.

Who is your competition? Other homeowners and real estate agents.

Let's face it, in your community, there are many houses for sale. Real Estate Agents are selling houses, other do-it-yourselfers are selling their houses and now you want to sell your house.

WOW, right? All this competition-how are you going to stand out?

We have your back as like I said before, we will teach you how to be different. When you are different, your competition fades away fast.

So get ready for the simplest and most effective way to sell your house starting right now!

Take out a notepad-take notes, turn off your cell phone, eliminate all distractions, and let's dive in! Let's take a bird view look at the whole process at selling your own house!

Steps to Selling a House Fast

1. Get The Price Right

2. Get The House Ready To Sell

3. Be Ready To Receive Buyer Phone Calls

4. Locate Potential Buyers

5.   Pre-screen Potential Buyers

6.   Meet With Buyer And Show Your House

7.   Schedule Closing With An Attorney

As you can see there are 7 steps that must be done to sell your house quickly.

CHAPTER 2

Which Selling Strategy is Right for You?

Before we dive in, we need to discuss selling strategies. There are three (3) main strategies to sell your house and they all revolve around how you want to be paid. Of course, we would all love to be cashed out but depending on your situation and timeframe for selling your house, considering other options is a good idea and it has increased the odds of our clients selling their house and it will do the same for you!

As a disclaimer, depending on which state your live in, be sure to ask your real estate attorney about these different options as they will require different paperwork, and laws may be different from state to state!

Here are the 3 main payment strategies you can use:

1.   **Cash Out** – This is where you will get cashed out or one lump sum when you sell your house. This is the most preferred payment sellers want. An example of this is if you want to sell your house for $100,000, you get paid $100,000 at closing.

2.   **Lease Option** - (Rent to own) If you have a current mortgage and need the payments to be covered, this strategy may work for you. A lease option is where the buyer agrees to pay your mortgage payment to the bank and is in charge of most maintenance and repairs on your home. In this option, somebody will rent your house for a predetermined time frame until they agree to cash you out by applying for a loan and paying the remaining balance off.

The benefit of this is if you have a mortgage on your house and you just need your mortgage payment made, and you find a buyer that can offer your monthly payments, you can still sell your house on a lease option agreement. This is sometimes a preferred method if in the rare case you can't find a buyer that will pay you full price in the time frame you need to sell.

An example of this type of selling strategy is as follows;

Situation- The homeowner needs to sell their house because they need to move due to a job transfer. They have 30 days to move to the new location.

Solution Option-They use the marketing methods mentioned in this program and they find a buyer that can pay them monthly on a lease purchases because they either can't qualify for a loan due to tightened lending standards by banks or they haven't built up their credit to get a loan from a bank yet.

The seller agrees to take monthly payments for their equity and pre-screens the buyer checking to see employment history and receiving a 10% down payment on the house.

The numbers would look like;

The selling price of the house is $100,000 and the buyer agrees to pay the seller $1,600 per month. The lease term is 10 years, which means the buyer will get a loan from a bank and cash the seller out within a 10 year period. The buyer puts down $10,000 as a deposit on the house.

Depending on your state laws, we recommend you talk to a Real Estate Attorney to discuss this option and what is involved in selling your house in this manner.

The seller is now receiving $1,600 per month and received a $10,000 deposit on the house. The $10,000 ensures that they have a good tenant buyer in their house. Within 10 years, as the agreement states, the buyer will qualify for a loan and pay you the remaining principle owed to you. This is very important point. Let me say it again, within the allotted time frame (lease term) you choose with the buyer, they will get qualified for a loan and cash you out of the remaining balance of your house.

You request a high down payment because the buyers that put down large down payments are more like homeowners. They have "skin in the game" if you will. This makes sure you have a quality tenant living in your house.

3.   **Owner Finance** - If you own your home free and clear, you can take back a note on the home. This means, someone will pay you monthly payments for the house. Picture this like you financed a car through a bank. In this example, you will be the bank and charging an interest rate. If you don't need all the cash up front, the benefit to this is you can actually get more for your house if you seller finance it because you are charging interest of 8-12%. When we sell a house by seller financing it, we usually make double the value of the house. But in this case, it is over a 10-20 year period.

This owner financing method works well if the buyer cannot get a loan through a traditional bank, but can still afford monthly payments. The same buyer in the lease purchase situation is also a perfect candidate for a seller financing deal.

The numbers are almost the same as the lease purchase deal with more thing-a great interest rate of 8-12%. Most buyers know that if they seller finance through a private party, they will be charged a higher interest rate than a bank would charge. You will be providing a service to someone charge what it is worth-8-12%.

You may be open to all three options depending on your situation or you may only pick one. Whatever you choose is great because you will know your situation best and what you want as a seller.

Having options does increase your chances to sell your house faster because you will be able to provide options to different buyers. Not everyone can pay all cash for a house, but they may be able to pay you monthly for your house. You decide which is best for you and your situation.

As you can see, this book is a little different. Most books on the market are all about selling for all cash and full price. But in reality and through our experience, that sometimes doesn't happen so I wanted to expose you to options you can choose from. Again, this book is about selling your house fast and one part of it is making it easy for the buyer to buy your house and potentially catering to all types of buyers.

CHAPTER 3

Types of Buyers

There are two types of buyers-cash buyers/investors and retail buyers. It is important to know the difference because your marketing message will be different for each buyer. Throughout this book you will notice we give you the message you will be using in your marketing efforts and the best part is that it attracts both types of buyers.

Let's review each buyer:

Cash buyer / Investor: This type of buyer pays cash for houses. We at Eau Claire Home Buyers are cash investors. But, we can only pay a certain price because we also repair houses to resell them to a retail buyer. Cash buyers buy houses as an investment and plans to make money from the property.

Cash Buyers don't want to live in the houses they buy. When selling to a cash buyer, they can close in as little as 3 days so it is the fastest way to get a pay check. On the flip side of that, you will not get full market value for your house when dealing with cash buyers. Cash buyers mostly deal with sellers that need to sell their house now, not only want to sell. If you have an ugly house that is need of serious repairs, and you can't afford to repair them yourself and you need to get out fast, a cash investor buyer is your buyer.

Let's recap the Pro's / Con's of Cash Buyers:

Pro's
- They pay cash at a reasonable price
- They don't take out loans to buy the house as they use their cash to buy houses
- They can close in 30 days, no waiting for banks
- They buy houses "as is" that need a lot of repair work, no inspections
- They can provide you options such as buying your house through lease purchase or seller financing

Con's
- They will not be able to pay you full market value because they will be also paying to repair the house to sell it to a retail buyer

Retail Buyers: This type of buyer looks to live in the house they buy. They usually apply for a loan from a bank to get the cash to buy the house. Retail buyers will pay market value but the sale may come delayed because they have to get a bank loan. Retail buyers will pay more but close slower on your house due to banks needing to get inspections done or anything else done before they loan the buyer money for the house.

Retail buyers also take longer to find as they are "shoppers" and look around at other options. Whereas investors, leap on a opportunity quickly and will be able to pay cash in 3 days. If you have a pretty house and your house doesn't need repairs, a retail buyer is usually your buyer unless you wish to go the lease purchase or seller financing route-then a investor can help you with this!

Let's recap the Pro's and Con's of Retail Buyers-

Pro's
- They will pay market value
- They will live in the house-they will be buying off emotions (discussed later in the program)
- They usually can get a bank loan so they can cash you out
- If they can't get a bank loan, they may be able to offer you monthly payments for your equity.
- They buy off emotion and we will be teaching you how to trigger your buyers emotions to increase the odds they will buy your house.

Con's
- It will take longer for them to close due to qualifying for a loan and anything else the banks needs to do before they lend the buyer money.
- They are shoppers as they will visit many houses before they make a final discussion on which house to buy

Now that you have an understanding of each buyer, lets dive into our next chapter-Get the Price Right

CHAPTER 4

Get the Price Right!

Pricing a home is a delicate process. You must decide this before you start marketing your house for sale. For the average homeowner, it isn't hard to price your house yourself. If in doubt, you can always hire an appraiser to get the market value of your house.

There are three priorities you must consider before you determine a selling price.

Priority 1 is to pay off your loan or any liens if you have some attached to the property. For example, if you owe $50,000 on your house, sell your house for more than $50,000. We recommend that you always sell your house at a price that will pay off all liens or loans attached to your property.

Priority 2 is to make it easy to buy through different options as we discussed above.

Priority 3 is you also want your home to be priced to sell quickly. To make a clear point, if you are asking full price and will not budge lower, it may be slower for you to sell your house.

The good news is that for every house, there is a buyer. But, finding that buyer may take some time.

Let's face it, we always want to get the most we can for our house right? Of course. Homeowners also need to realize, that buyers want a good deal as well and when they believe they are getting a deal, the faster they will decide buy your house!

The biggest thing homeowners must think about is the total "value" of your house. And think of the value from the *buyer's perspective*.

For example; if your house is worth $100k and you are asking $110k but your house needs a new roof and the water heater needs to be replaced, it may be hard for you to sell your house at that price point.

Why?

Because the buyer may be looking at how much it will cost to fix the roof and replace water heater. And since it is not hard to figure out a ball park value of what the house is worth, they may think you are asking too much.

With that said, once you know the value of your house you need to take into consideration the possible repairs or anything else that the buyer may see as an expense. Then, price your house fairly.

When deciding on the value of your house, you will need to get comparable sales data for the area you live in. This means, you will need to see what houses sold for in your area that are similar to your own house. By doing this, you will get a good idea what your house is worth.

But...Remember, your house is worth what the market will pay and in the timeframe you have it up for sale.

For example, if you own a $100,000 house and you put it up for sale for 6 months and the most buyers will offer you is $70,000, the market values your home at $70,000. Comparable sales data is what houses has sold for so the data is from the past. As real estate markets change, the past may not equal the future. This can work in your favor or not. It all depends on the current real estate market.

The point we want to is you will need to get the comparable sales data for your house in the area your property is located and then know that is only a target number to try for.

You may get less or more when the final sale goes through! We want you to get the most you can get but the main reason why people don't sell their houses fast is because they get greedy and want only top dollar. Most of the time, these sellers don't understand why they can't sell their house and it stays on the market for years.

The best place to get comparable sales data is from a Real Estate Agent, but with asking something from an agent, they may ask you to list with them. If you do not want to, you don't have to. The majority of agents will help you out!

When talking to a Realtor, all you need to ask them is,
"Can you please pull comparable sales for my house at 123 Main St. City, State".

Once they do this, they can give you a rough estimate of what your house is worth.

This estimated value of your house is assuming there is not any major needed repairs on the house and if there are, they are very small such as new carpet or a new toilet. This estimated value is assuming also that your house is in similar condition as the other houses that have sold in your area.

If your house needs a new roof, that would skew the value that the agent gives you. The value of your house would technically be lower in the buyers eyes.

We use a couple online services as well to help us get an estimated value of a house we are trying to sell. There are many sites such as Zillow.com or Eapprasial.com you can use to find comparable sales data.

Quick tip: Here is a Two-Step Question Series we use to get the most for our houses we sell and you can use it to for your house!

See below:

Selling Tip Worth Up To $5,719.00

(We made an extra $5,719 using this tip alone when we sold a house, you can do the same)

When you begin talking to buyers (We will discuss this later in the program) and they are interested in buying your house…

Always ask the buyer, **"What's the most you can pay?"**

Follow up with asking, **"Is that the best you can do?"**

If the buyer likes your home, they can always come up with more money. If you ask these questions, you WILL get the best price. You need to ask these questions with authority and in disbelief. The second question should be said in a way that you don't believe them so they feel pressure to increase the price if they want the home.

Just to make sure you understand, the speed of your house selling is in direct proportion to the value you are giving to the buyer! And it is all determined in your buyer.

Another thing to mention here is using a simple mind trick. We like numbers like $109,577 or $107,599. Numbers that end with a 7 or 9 make the brain think you are paying a lower cost for an item. Simple, yet effective.

CHAPTER 5

Staging the House for Sale

Before you tell the world your house is for sale - it may be smart to do some housekeeping.

Picture this stage of selling your house like washing your clothes before you have a garage sale. The purpose of a garage sale is to sell your stuff right? And you want your merchandise looking good so people will want to buy it!

What is often unknown to homeowners is that buyers buy off emotion when deciding to buy your house, so when a buyer walks into your home, they should feel like it's home and they need to be able to visualize their belongings in your house.

Buyers buy off emotion first, and then use logic to back it up so you must appeal to their emotions right away. It isn't hard to do this as we will show you soon!

Picture this for a moment:

A couple walks into a TV store and looks to buy a TV for their family. This couple has 2 kids and they love watching movies as a family. They find a TV at a good price and decide to purchase it.

What do you think the driving motivation was to buy a TV? Was it the features of the TV? The size? Or the price?

Nope!

What the couple was envisioning when they were looking at TV's was the family time they would have with their kids watching a movie on a Friday night. They were picturing going to the movie store, picking out a movie, making popcorn, sitting the kids on the couch, turning down the lights, and turning on a new family movie all the while looking at their kid's faces glow in excitement!

They bought the TV because of the emotions they felt.

But what happens when the Husband is asked why he bought the TV?

He may say something like, "Oh, I got it at a great price, it's 52 inches with ultra-definition. And it will be great to watch movies with my kids! We always have family night on Fridays!"

What happened here? He used logic to back up his decision to buy the TV. This is what happens every time someone buys anything.

By knowing this, you now have the upper hand to appeal to your buyers emotions when selling your house!

Depending on your circumstance, whether your house is vacant or occupied, some ideas may not fit your situation but I still wanted to include everything I could.

If your house is vacant, you can really have fun with this as it is easiest to sell a vacant nice looking house. This is because homebuyers like clean empty houses because they can visualize their belongings in the house!

If you still live in the house, no problem, try to clean it up the best you can and take as much stuff out of it and into your new house or storage unit. We recommend this because from the hundreds of buyers we have spoken to-they are more inclined to buy a house if it is practically empty.

If this doesn't fit your situation-don't worry. Clean it up the best you can and still do the things we are about to share with you! Always make the best of your situation.

Here is a list of what needs to be done before you tell the world your house is for sale. We have tested these and found that we sell houses faster by staging our houses like this!

Bathroom

- Put new shower curtains in your bathroom-keep the color plain to appeal to many buyers
- Put towels on the hanger
- Put wash clothes in the cabinets
- Always put on a new roll of toilet paper-Just like a hotel does
- Put a throw rug in front of the sink, neutral colors work best
- Put some flowers on the toilet top

Kitchen

- Put a small plant on the counter top
- Fold the towels and fill the paper towel holder
- The counter tops should be emptied and clean except for kitchen appliances. New home owners like to visualize their stuff on the counter tops.
- Put a nice rug in front of the sink like the bathroom
- Make sure the sink is very clean
- Put nice curtains on the windows if applicable

Living Room

- Depersonalize all pictures on walls (take down), again the new buyer will want to put up their own pictures.
- Put a nice-welcoming rug in front of doorway
- Feel free to put new plants by the doorway to make it more welcoming
- If you have a fireplace-Clean it, a topper is acceptable.

Lawn

- Cut and clean your lawn or any bushes in your yard
- Make sure all clutter is eliminated and all garbage is pick up
- Make sure all garbage cans are emptied

For you guys out there…

If you're a guy, let your wife or girlfriend stage the house. Guy's don't stage very well. We don't seem have the eye for it!

Don't forget the outside of your house is just as important as the inside of your house. Make sure the outside is looking clean and looking the best it can. When your buyer looks at your house for the first time, you want them to have a good feeling about what they are seeing!

Always put yourself in the buyers place. We recommend driving around your neighborhood and rate the houses you see on a scale of 1-10 with 10 being great looking.

Next time you drive to the store, look at houses and remember what you don't like and what you do like as if you were looking in your neighborhood for a house to buy. This will give you a great idea on what buyers are looking for!

Notice: If your home has any <u>structural</u> or <u>foundation issues</u>, you will want to repair them prior to the sale of your home. As buyers stop by to see the home, they will notice this potential money pit and if they need to qualify for a loan at a bank, the home will need to be inspected prior to the bank giving the buyer a loan for the property which may delay the sale of the house.

If you use the owner finance method, you may be able to slide past fixing these repairs yourself. Just make sure you write in the purchase and sales agreement (we always recommend working with a real estate attorney to write up and close the transaction and you can request them to write this in the Standard Purchase and Sales Agreement or any other document your state requires) that these repairs or damages were presented to the buyer and the buyer accepts responsibility for fixing these issues upon successful purchase of the property.

When you have completed as much as you can do- we are getting closer to having some fun marketing your house to the world. But first, we need to figure out how you will handle all the calls from potential buyers!

CHAPTER 6

Be Ready To Receive Buyer Phone Calls

Picture this for a moment…

You put up several yard signs in high traffic areas around your city that say you want to sell your house and within one hour, you get 50 calls. With each call, you must explain every aspect of your house and answer questions and you realize at the end of the day, all these people just wanted to inquire about the house and not buy it!

How would you feel?

Well this was what happened when we started investing in houses. We spent hours on the phone spinning our wheels talking to people that really didn't want to buy the house. It was a waste of time!

Many of our private clients experience this as well before they hired us to coach them to sell their own house. We do not want this to happen to you! We created a system to prevent this from ever happening to anyone!

After we wasted a lot of time talking to buyers, we got a little smarter! We realized our time was being wasted by "tire-kickers" just inquiring where we could have just posted everything about the house online and then have only seriously interested buyers call us! What a brainstorm right?

We are going to teach you a process called pre-screening and it will save you a lot of time and headaches!

Pre-screening is the act of giving the information to somebody and letting them decide if they are interested in moving forward. This way, when somebody calls you, you know they have viewed information on your house and based on that information, they are seriously interested in looking further into it.

In reference to the above example, can you imagine if all of those 50 callers were serious buyers in the first hour -after we put out the signs? We would have had a verbal agreement to buy the house in 8 hours!

This is how powerful this is and this is one secret most home sellers don't even think about! But, you will have the upper hand now by knowing this and that's why you now have the advantage in your marketplace!

So where do you post information about your house?

You will create a simple website for free! At Wordpress.com.

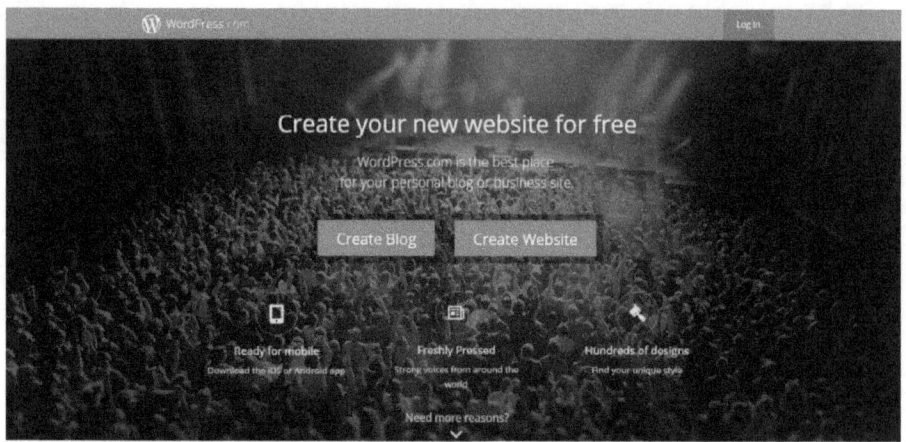

All you have to do is click over to Wordpress.com and sign up. The site will walk you through what you need to do to set up a simple website including the site name, template and configuration.

Don't worry about how the site looks as the only thing that will be important to the website is the content-which is your house's information. You will want the house to stand out so a plain-template website is best.

You will notice when you first create your website it will ask for a site address which is the domain name. For example, we have used "houseforsaleeauclaire.wordpress.com" We will usually put "houseforsale" and then our current city the house is in "Eau Claire".

This will make it easy to tell someone the web address to look at the details of your house.

After you set up your initial simple website- you will need to fill it with content about your house. If you would like me to personally walk you through the setup of the website, please visit the url below;

http://eauclairehomebuyers.com/**bonuscontent/**

Below is a rough template of what you may want to add to your website. I have included notes in the template to personalize it to your house and city! All you have to do is change what it says by adding your houses characteristics and information!

_____Top_____

For Sale By Owner-Must Sell Fast $109,977
123 Main St. MyCity, St. MyZip
Priced to sell quickly-Discounted $11,984
Call Mitch Directly at 555-555-5555 if you are interesting in Purchasing!

DESCRIPTION: (Feel free to add your own description. Describe the property as if you had to sell it over the phone)
Cute and charming house located 10 miles from City, State. A Handy Man's Dream-Spiff and Shine needed!

* Large backyard
* Mature Maple Trees-Perfect for Maple syrups
* Large Attached two car garage
* Excellent Condition Roof
* Backyard utility shed with electricity
* Large Back Deck for family cookouts

- Large Picture Window
- Nearby Schools-City High School, Name of school Elementary School

PROPERTY FEATURES

- Built in 1965
- 3 bed 1 bath
- 980 square foot
- 1 acre back yard
- Living room
- Storage space
- Pantry
- Basement
- Mud room
- Refrigerator
- Balcony, Deck, or Patio
- Yard
- Lawn
- Ceiling fans
- Large backyard
- Mature Maple Trees-Perfect for Maple syrups
- Large Attached two car garage
- Excellent Condition Roof
- Backyard utility shed with electricity
- Large Back Deck for family cookouts
- Large Picture Window
- Nestled by Schools-Durand High School, Arkansas Elementary School

COMMUNITY FEATURES

- Garage - Attached

ADDITIONAL LINKS

- Website: http:houseforsaleeauclaire.wordpress.com

Contact info:
Mitch and Matt Hell
EauClaireHomeBuyers.com
555-555-5555

_____Bottom_____
Anything you feel would be important to a buyer should be included.

After you get all the information on your new website, now you need to add pictures to your website so people can view it. You should add a picture to your website as shown above.

What Matt and I also use is Flickr.com. The best thing is Flickr.com is easy to use and it is very self-explanatory!

You will need to take pictures of all sides of your house, if you have a yard take pictures of all aspects of the yard, take pictures of all rooms as well.

You will want to create an account on Flickr.com and upload all the pictures you took. Name the new folder the address of your house.

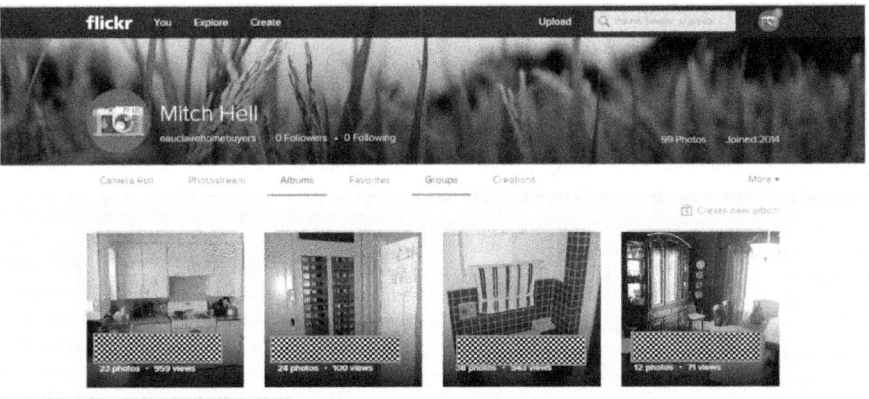

After you have uploaded the your house pictures to Flickr.com, save the url of the album for reference; See below

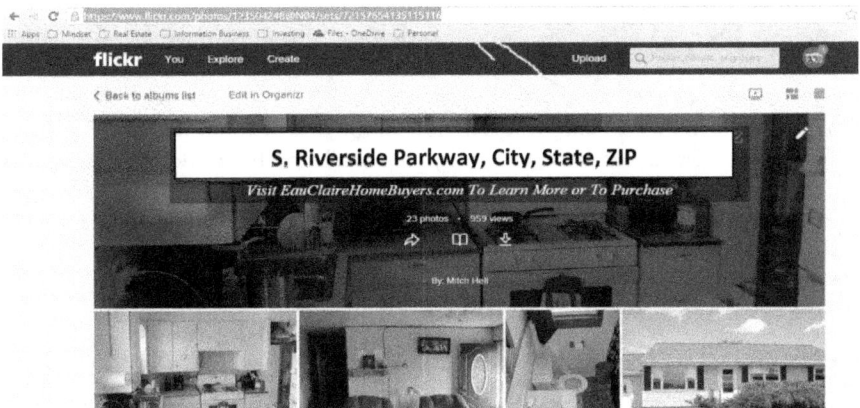

Depending on how technical you are; you can either link this url to your website as a hyperlink or you can save this url for when buyers call you and want to see more pictures, you can forward this url in an email to them.

For now, this will be as technical as it gets so I don't confuse anyone. I know when I first started, websites scared me and the learning process was slow so I begged my mentors for an easy way to do things!

So to keep this simple-If a buyer calls you and is interested in your house, and wants to see even more pictures of the house ask for their email and send them this link and they can view it!

I would recommend you upload some pictures of the house to the WordPress site such as the front of the house, back of the house, side of the house, living room, kitchen, bathroom, and basement.

At this point, you have a new website and you have a new Flickr account! Make sure you save both the url's. The "url" is the web address such as http://eauclairehomebuyers.com. You will need these when you market your house online to drive a lot of buyers your way!

Now, when somebody calls you, all you have to say is go to my WordPress site at (Your site name). Now you can save time on the phone and have your potential buyer look at your house for themselves and decide if they want to buy it or not.

An example of a phone call would be;

Ring, Ring, Ring

You-Hello?

Buyer-Yeah, I am calling about the house for sale. Can you tell me more about it?

You-Thank you for calling, you can view all the details about the house at (your site name). If you are interested in it, please call me back and we can discuss details!

Buyer-Oh great, thank you!

You-Bye

Buyer-Bye

By doing it this way, you will not be on the phone for hours telling everyone about your house. You are making it easy for someone to make a decision to look further into your house by calling you!

Setting this system up usually takes only 20 minutes, and solves 3 very big challenges most home sellers face:

1.)   It will save you time from saying the same thing over and over again on the phone.

2.)   It will pre-screen buyers and the ones that call you back are the ones that are actually interested-increasing your odds of the sale of your house.

3.)   It makes it easy for the buyer to make a decision because all the information is in one place.

As you can see, this is very different than the "standard" way most people sell their house! We are simplifying it and showing you what we do to sell houses fast in today's market!

CHAPTER 7

Marketing Your House for Sale

Just so you know, I am jumping off my computer chair-so excited to talk about marketing. This is my specialty and I love teaching other homeowners about it! What makes me so excited is that I know the power of marketing houses and how effective it is to get a lot of potential buyers your way.

It all comes down to this;

"When you want to sell your house fast, the more people looking at your house, the faster the sale. So your marketing must be smart, effective and cost-effective."

To make sure we are all on the same page, I want to cover what Marketing means. What I have realized throughout our consulting sessions with homeowners is that some homeowners don't understand what marketing actually means.

Marketing can be broken down to three aspects;

"The correct message...to the correct market...delivered through the correct media"
The correct message is what you are doing-Selling your house.

The correct market is-Cash buyers and retail buyers looking to buy houses.

The correct media is how you advertise your house for sale through the marketing methods we will be talking about shortly. Media refers to where you will advertise your house for sale such as Craigslist.com or a newspaper.

What makes marketing effective is advertising your message to the people, where they are already looking for what they want-media.

Here is an example;

Situation: You have a house for sale

Your Message: House For Sale-Must Sell Fast

Your Market: Anyone looking to buy a house-Cash Buyers or Retail Buyers as we discussed the attributes earlier in this book.

Your Advertising Media: You know buyers are always looking for houses on Craiglist.com so you place a carefully crafted advertisement on Craistlist.com to attract buyers to your house.

Here's the kicker-We give you everything you need. We give you the message in this program, the market, and the media that are best for selling houses quickly!

I will be teaching you four primary methods for selling houses quickly in Today's market.

Strategy #1-Craigslist.com

We like Craigslist because it's the most popular local selling website and people trust it.

We are going to show you the simplest and **proven way** to **sell your house at light speed on Craigslist**!

Most homeowners we meet usually know to place a craigslist advertisement to market their house for sale. They also place a For Sale By Owner sign in their yard to draw in potential buyers. At that point, homeowners usually stop their marketing efforts and see if they can get a buyer.

We want to share with you some proven and tested strategies you can use on Craigslist.com that will supercharge your advertisements and to help you find a buyer as quick as possible. As most people know, Craigslist is a great place to buy and sell stuff and many people use Craigslist to find what they are looking for, including houses!

What you will want to do is either sign up or sign into your Craigslist.com account. After you do that, make sure you are under your current city your house is located. For example, the url will look like this; eauclaire.craigslist.org if your current city is Eau Claire WI.

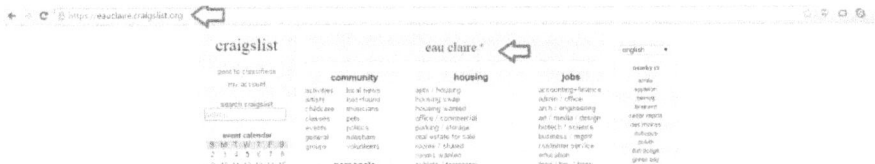

After you do that, click on the section that says "Post To Classifieds"

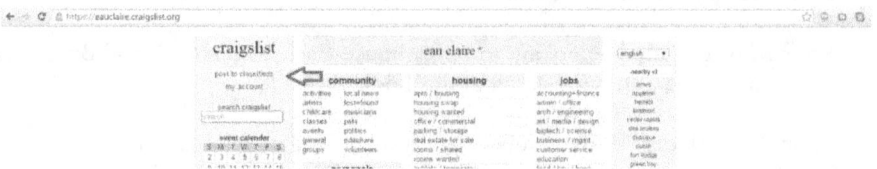

Next, you will be prompted to pick from several categories to clarify where you want to list your advertisement. We recommend listing your house under the "housing offered" category and/or the services category under real estate.

See the picture below

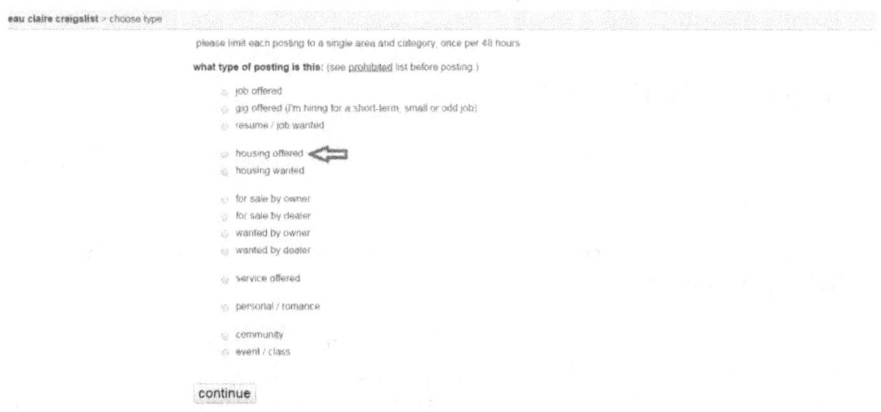

Once you have successfully completed the above steps, select the "Real Estate-By Owner" option and then you will be at the place you will need to post your ad. See the picture below for reference.

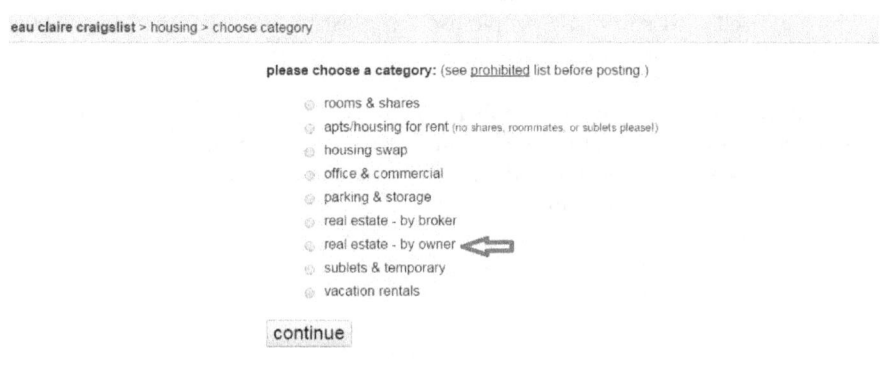

Here is a picture of what it should look like when you are at the page you start to enter your advertisement to sell your house.

posting title		specific location	postal code	

posting body   please enter phone numbers as contact info above, not in posting body below.

posting details

open house dates

ft²	price	available on	bedrooms	bathrooms
0	$	aug ▼ 5	0 ▼	- ▼

housing type	laundry	parking
apartment ▼	- ▼	- ▼

furnished   no smoking   wheelchair accessible

show on maps

street	optional
cross street	optional
city	

ok for others to contact you about other services, products or commercial interests

continue

Here is a step by step process to posting an effective advertisement.

Step One: When you place your ads on Craigslist.com follow the example below;

Title: MUST SELL FAST-DESPERATE SELLER-Discounted $XXX (If you can discount your house a bit, state how much you reduced the price.) Even if you are not desperate, state it anyway. When buyers see the word desperate, it will trigger them to look at the house and that is half the battle with Craigslist advertising. Your title of your post is meant to draw attention and to get a potential buyer to click to learn more about your house.

Location: This is self-explanatory, fill in your location of your house.

Description: Write a short description of the highlights of your property such as Price, Bed, Bath, Location, Yard Size, Square Footage, etc. **You must include the url of your website and flickr account** so people can see the full description. Your description is where your potential buyer will learn more about the house and then make a decision to further explore their options for buying it or not.

An example of the description would be:

House for sale
Must sell Fast $109,977
3 bed 2 bath
1500 square foot, 1 acre
My City, My State
Visit (yoursitename).wordpress.com for details
and view (flickr url) for pictures!

(At the time of this writing, I am able to add my url to my description. As the internet changes, there may be limits to what you can do and how you promote using your url's. If that has happened, and you are not allowed to post your url in the description box, simply put the word "DOT" where your (.) period is before the "com" portion of your url. For example, it would look like this; EauClaireHomeBuyersDOTcom.)

Step Two: Place your ad in as many areas of Craigslist as you can that makes sense. For example, put it in housing offered, community, real estate wanted and others that are related to anything real estate or home buying.

Step Three: So your ad is on Craigslist, now what? To maximize your exposure, you will need to re-write your ad 4-5 different times. For example, here is a couple examples of different headlines you will want to copy:

1.)   MUST SELL MY HOUSE FAST-I AM DESPERATE
2.)   DESPERATE SELLER- WIFE/HUSBAND IS MAKING ME SELL OUR HOUSE
3.)   HOME BUYERS WANTED-DESPERATE SELLER- MUST SELL HOUSE
4.)   DISCOUNTED HOUSE-MUST SELL FAST CALL 555-555-5555

The reason why you want to re-write your ad several times is because you are now going to post your ad (each time a different version of your ad) every 3 days. This will keep your post current and on top of the search status as people look for homes to buy. The reason why you need to re-write your ad is because craigslist will delete your ad if the same ad is posted too often. How do you think we know that? Trial and Error my friends!

Strategy #2-Using Facebook

Facebook can be a highly targeted way to advertise your home for sale. The best thing about Facebook is it is a social network that allows other people to connect in one place. Facebook users take advantage of this by forming "groups".

There are many different kinds of groups people can join but there is a great group in most cities that people can post items to sell, including houses.

To find a group like this in your city or nearest city, simply search in the Facebook search box, "(Your current city) stuff for sale".

For example, if you live in Eau Claire, WI, you would search "Eau Claire Stuff For Sale".

We have an "Eau Claire for sale group" that we advertise in. It has nearly 38,000 members and when we post houses, we get a massive response.

There may be many different types of groups in relation to selling stuff in your local city and if there are many of them, join all of them and do this process in all of them.

Once you join the group, you will want to post your house for sale in it!

All you have to do is post the price, property address and description, good photos of the home and your website address and post. Pretty much the same as your Craigslist.com ad.

You will get comments and messages on your house from interested buyers shortly after you post (if your group is large) and you will want to respond to each appropriately.

Another option on Facebook is If you have a large friends list and people are already "liking" what you post on Facebook, post your house to your Facebook timeline.

The reason why this is so important is your Facebook friends can share your post and they can expose your house to many other people in their network of friends.

The secret to this is to ask people to share your house on your post.

An example of this is;

Mitch Hell
June 7 at 6:30pm · Edited · ⚐ ▾

Discounted House For Sale!
S. Riverside Parkway, City, State, ZIP

Handyman Special-3 bed, 1 bath-Spiff and shine needed! $69,000 Cash Only. After repaired Value $110,399- Priced To Sell, Discounted $41,399.
Please share and like this post to spread the word on this great deal!
Visit http://eauclairehomebuyers.com/housesforsale/
For more information

Like · Comment · Share · 👍 5 💬 2 ↗ 8

(Address and house hidden for privacy purposes)

This is an example of a property we could sell at a discount. Note that we asked people to share and like my Facebook Post to help spread the word on my house for sale. So far, after 1 hour this post was up, I have 8 shares, 2 comments and 5 likes.

Within 1 day, we had people calling to buy the property! We sold the property in 13 days to a person who found our house for sale on Facebook through one of the people that shared my post!

It works!

When you post to Facebook, follow these steps:

1) Create a catchy title that your audience will like such as; Help me sell my house, I am selling my house, House For Sale, Need to sell my house because... Wife making me sell...., etc.

2) Post a little bit out the house and the price. If you are selling it at a discount, include the real price of it and how much you are discounting it.

3) Add your website link in the post so people can follow that link to see full details.

4) Post a picture of it. The best picture you have of the front of the house including the yard if you have it.

5) Ask your following to share and like the post.

6) When someone does like and share your post-THANK THEM in the comments to influence more of a sharing frenzy!

Strategy #3-Yard Signs

Yard signs are by far the best way to get the word out that you are selling your house. Most home sellers know this but they don't seem to know the entire story. Most, put a For Sale By Owner sign in their yard and then that's it. Maybe the put another sign down the road.

I will tell you this....that is not how you use yard signs.

When you use yard signs the correct way, you will have people calling you the same day or next day. And you will thank me for telling you about the "pre-screening" process I explained earlier.

How do you use large signs correctly?

First, you will NOT be using a "For Sale By Owner" sign. If you have one, put it in your garage. It's boring and doesn't work in regards to selling your house quickly. Everyone uses this so most home buyers are conditioned to overlook the sign.

Let me ask you, the last time you drove to work, have you ever noticed a new billboard or sign advertisement that you didn't see before? I bet you have but after a while, you see the sign so often, you don't even notice it anymore. This happens all the time. When people see the same thing over and over again, our brains become immune to it so we don't actually sense that we see them anymore.

Somehow, and I am going to show you soon, you need to "Shock" people so they wake up from their unconscious sleep and make them look at your house for sale!

Somehow you need to get people that are driving by your house to take a second look at your house because your yard is so bizarre and different. Home buyers must think they are missing out on something if they don't look at your house!

Let's dive in on how to create this amazing effect!

You will need to make your house look like a carnival so it draws massive attention by putting yard signs that are different colors in your yard. These signs should state the main points of your house such as price, bed/bath and if you are offering a discount.

See the picture below.

This will draw attention and will get people talking. Why? Because nobody does this and that is to your benefit. Doing something odd is the best marketing method because it draws attention! Feel free to add balloons or anything that makes it look fun and exciting!

The next thing you will want to do pepper your neighborhood with colored yard signs. You can buy all your material at a dollar store! You can buy some yellow paint to spray paint the white board if they don't sell Yellow or other bright colored boards. Then, *handwrite* the sign and pepper your neighborhood with the signs. Put the yard signs in all high traffic areas.

TIP: Using a corrugated board is best if you live in a rainy state.

And here is another BIG secret-Make your signs ugly! Make sure people can read your handwriting, but make it ugly. Our best signs, were so darn ugly, it looked like a 3rd grader wrote them.

The reason why you want your signs hand written and ugly is they are authentic and original and people emotionally respond to original things.

You will also want to put out pointer signs on the road you live on. Use the pointer signs on your road to point people to your house. Don't put pointer signs around a city if your house is not located close to the pointer signs.

Think of marketing a garage sale. You want people to come so you put a pointer sign at an intersection that points them to your house. It's the same thing here!

I would recommend putting out 30 signs a week depending on how large your city or town is. If your city or town is bigger, you may want to put more out to cover more ground.

Below we show some examples of signs and pointer signs for reference.

Must Sell
3 Bed, 2 Bath
$109,977
555-555-5555

Must Sell
3 Bed 2 Bath

$109,977
555-555-5555

*Strategy #4 U*se a Video Tour and Youtube.com

Creating a video tour of your house is a nice way to promote your house for sale online. It will help your potential buyer make a decision easier as they will be able to see the house without having to go to it.

People are busy nowadays and before people make a commitment to look further into something, they need a good reason too. This is all geared toward making it easier for the buyer.

It is very easy to create a video tour. All you need to use is your smart phones video camera. If you don't have a smartphone, use can use an external video camera.

What you will want to do is stand in front of the house and hold your camera at face level. Start the video and steadily record the front of the house and then rotating it from left or right. Feel free to turn completely around to view the neighborhood. As you complete the frontal area, take a walk of the backyard.

Keep the video recording going the entire time. Move slowly and record everything you can. Feel free to explain highlights or concerns about the house on the video so people know what they are looking at.

Next, step into the house and do the same. Record each room, steadily and slowly so people can really get a good picture of it. With each room you enter, say the name of the room and something nice about it.

Once you are done with your video tour, you will need to upload it to your computer. On most smartphones, you can plug your phone into the computer using the charging cord. From there, open and view the files on your phone, find the video and drag and drop it over to your desktop on your computer.

From there, upload it to Youtube.com. To upload a video, you will need to have a Gmail email address or account. Simply sign in to your account on Youtube.com and on the right upper corner of the webpage you will see "upload". Click that button and find your video on your computer.

When your video is uploading, you will be able to fill out some details about the video such as your Title and Description and Tags.

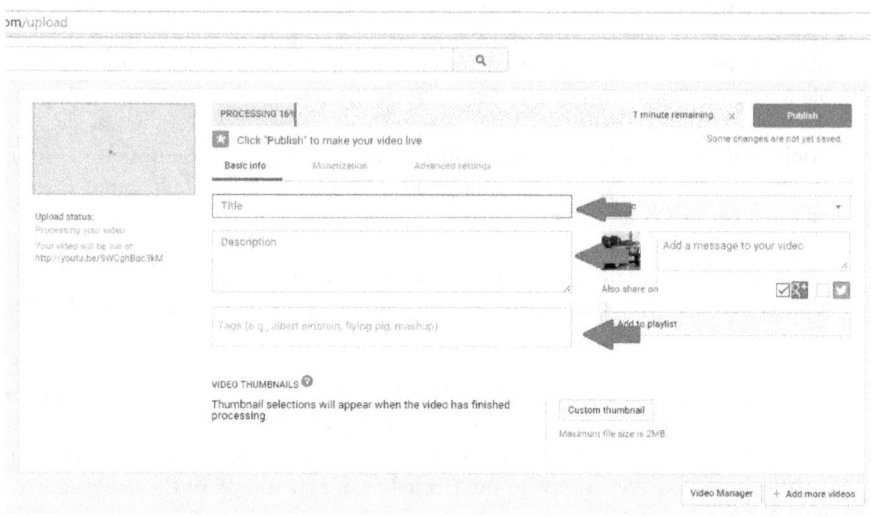

This process is the same as the Craigslist.com ads.

For the **Title section**-Use a title such as;

$$House For Sale-(Your City)-Must Sell Fast

For the **description section**-Simple fill out the same as the craigslist ad you wrote such as;

House for sale-(City)
Must sell Fast $109,977
3 bed 2 bath
1500 square foot, 1 acre
Visit (yoursitename).wordpress.com for details
and view (flickr url) for pictures!

You will also see a section that says "tags". In the **"tag" section,** type in words about your house so YouTube can help people find your video.

Words such as:

1.) House for sale (your city)
2.) (your city) sell house
3.) Buy House (your city)
4.) Houses for sale (your city)

Here is how it will look all filled out-See below

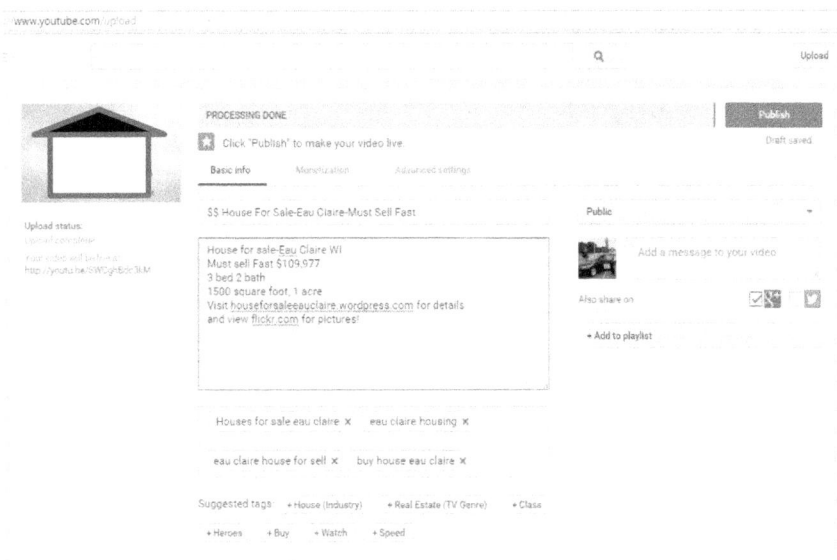

Once your video is uploaded and you have filled out all of your information, you can upload your video to your website if you wish or you can leave it from here.

What your video will do is pop up on search engines as people type in certain words.

For example, if I am new to town, I may type into Google.com- "Buy House in (city)"

When the search results load, your video may be on the first page and most people are drawn to view videos. This is a great way to promote your house for sale as people are looking to find houses online as well!

Here is an example how we are on the first page of google for that keyword with our video tours of a house we were selling at the time.

(Address hidden for privacy purposes)

 buy house eau claire

Web   Shopping   Maps   News   Images   More ▾   Search tools

About 31,500 results (0.91 seconds)

For Sale: 822 | WI Walk ...

www.youtube.com/watch?v=CW1JOhfiFPg
Aug 6, 2014 - Uploaded by Eau Claire Home Buyers
For Sale: 822 E Lowes Creek Rd Eau Claire WI Walk Through
INSIDE. Eau Claire Home Buyers ...

FOR SALE: 822   WI Walk ...

www.youtube.com/watch?v=BsdWUGdHa9A
Aug 6, 2014 - Uploaded by Eau Claire Home Buyers
FOR SALE: 822 E Lowes Creek Rd Eau Claire WI Walk
Through OUTSIDE. Eau Claire Home Buyers ...

We Buy Houses Eau Claire How To Sell Your House On ...

www.youtube.com/watch?v=YMf5KSv4euw
Apr 29, 2014 - Uploaded by Eau Claire Home Buyers
We Buy Houses Eau Claire How To Sell Your House On
Craigslist FAST ... For Sale: 822 E Lowes Creek Rd ...

Eau Claire Real Estate | Find Houses & Homes for Sale in ...
www.century21.com › Wisconsin ▾ Century 21 Real Estate ▾
764 Listings - Search Eau Claire real estate property listings to find homes for sale in
Eau Claire, WI. Browse ... Once in a lifetime opportunity to own this 11 acre estate on
Lowes Creek .... each with their own walk-in closets and full baths w/heated tiled
floors. ..... 66 Acres wooded with Beaver Creek flowing through property.

Eau Claire, WI Lake Property For Sale - LakePlace.com

CHAPTER 8

Pre-screen Potential Buyers

Once you have your marketing in place, it's time to wait for calls! Since you have set up your Pre-Screening system, you can feel confident that the calls you get are serious people that are interested in your house.

If a buyer calls you and has not look at your website (usually because your yard signs only have your phone number on it), simply refer them to your website to get all the details and to call you back if they are interested

One idea to mention is changing your voicemail to say;

"Hi, you have reached (name), I am currently away from my phone but if you leave a message, I will give you a call back. If you are calling about my house for sale, please visit (your city).worpress.com for more information"

This way, if you miss a call, buyers can still get the web address to your house to see full details.

When potential buyers call you back and are interested in seeing your house, you must ask them three very important questions that will pre-qualify them to see your house. After they have successfully answered the questions to your liking, only then you show the house to them.

What you do not want is people viewing your house and you spending time showing your house to find out that the buyer is not prequalified for a loan or doesn't have a down payment.

That is why you prequalify your buyer before you spend your precious time showing your house. You don't want to waste time talking to people that don't have any money. Would you agree?

The questions you must ask the buyer after they have viewed your website and called you back are as follows:

1.)   How will you finance my house?
2.)   Are you prequalified for a loan?
3.)   How much do you have for a down payment?

By asking these three questions, you will know if they have money or not. It is very important to know if they can pay for your house as you will have many people calling you once you starting using these marketing methods.

Let's review each questions so you know what to look for;

How will you finance my house?

What you want to hear is that they will get a loan from a bank or pay all cash for it. A serious buyer will know how they will buy a house. If they say, they don't know or they are thinking about a bank loan, simply ask them to get pre-qualified for a bank loan and call you back at a later date.

Are you prequalified for a loan?

Serious buyers will be pre-qualified for a loan because they need to know how much house they can afford and how much a month they will be paying. Serious buyers have already budgeted a house expense into their personal finances and now are looking for the actual house they plan to buy. If the potential buyer is not prequalified for a loan, as stated earlier, refer them back to the bank and tell them to call you when they are pre-qualified. Don't waste your time with people that are not serious.

How much do you have for a down payment?

Any buyer looking to purchase a house will have a sizable down payment ready. When asking how much they have, get the potential buyer to tell you a number. In our experience, anything less than 10% is a No Deal!

Why?

Because if someone can't come up with 10% and they are in the market to buy a house, they are usually not serious. The more of a down payment they have the more serious they are. Now, if they are getting a loan through a bank, the bank usually has asked this question already. And the money will go to the bank to be put against the principle amount. But this question is for your knowledge that you are speaking to a real buyer.

If the buyer doesn't want to tell you this information or any of the information described above, simply tell them that you are only interested in talking to and showing your house to serious buyers and if they can't provide you with the information, you are not interested in selling the house to them.

This is a selling technique that is called a take away close. You have a house they want to buy but since they don't cooperate on your terms, you take the house away. This will either get them to tell you or this will pre-qualified them out so you don't waste your time on "tire-kickers".

Once they say they have money to pay for your house, ask for a Proof of Funds. They can get this from their Bank or they can print you some other document that has the funds located on it.

You will be happy you are doing this because you will have the peace of mind knowing you are working with someone that has money or can get money to buy your house quickly.

CHAPTER 9

Meet With Buyer and Show Your House

Now it's time to meet with your potential buyer-how exciting! Schedule a time that works for you and block out around two hours of time. This will give you a cushion of time so you can answer any questions your buyers has and show them the house. As you can see, two hours of your time is a lot so you only want to spend time with serious buyers!

You are the best person to show your home to a potential buyer. So, when meeting with the buyer, make sure you show them everything they want to see. Leave nothing out. Be sure to show them anything that needs to be fixed in the future, because if they find out after closing that they was a potential problem, it may bite you in the rear later.

If the buyer would like to have a contractor look at any repairs, the buyer is responsible for paying the contractor to inspect your house. The same goes for any other professional services.

As you can see, we have not explained any negotiations with the buyer yet. The reason for this is we only sell our houses on our terms and we advise you do the same. We know when we first started buying and selling houses negotiations where very uncomfortable and we know from talking to homeowners, most homeowners try to avoid negotiations at all costs.

In your mind, change the word negotiations to just plain talking with the buyer. That is all that it is. And you must understand that buyers have concerns and are making a big decision and what they really want is a good deal and more "logic" to back up their buying decisions.

Picture the last time you bought something big such as a new TV. What people normally do is research what TV they want to buy. They will look on the internet and walk into BestBuy for example and ask a ton of questions.

In these buying moments, the buyer is looking for several reasons why they want to buy it or should buy it. They need the sales person to tell them how this TV will benefit their lives.

It all comes back to what I said before, people buy off emotion first, and then, back it up by logic. So, the people that want a new TV have an emotional connection to the TV for some reason and they pursue buying one. But their logic sets in and they want the best price, more features and more logical reasons to buy it so they question, they research, they ponder the decision until they finally pull the trigger and bring their new TV home for their family.

When you walk the potential buyer through your house, talk in a calm voice, but get excited to show what you really like about your house. Be completely honest and transparent with your buyer because if your buyer trusts you and believes you are being honest with him or her, the better the chance of any transaction to go through.

Using this system you will rarely negotiate because you will be able to cherry pick the buyers you want. Keep in the back of your mind, your buyer needs to impress you to sell them your house. This will give you the confidence to stand up and sell your house on your terms.

Picture two different scenarios;

1.)   You didn't read this book before venturing of to sell your house and you put a For Sale By Owner sign in your yard and you wait....and wait...and a couple people call you. You show your house and then one is interested in calling you. You talk to the buyer and the buyer doesn't agree to your terms or price. How do you deal with this?

This is a situation you will need to negotiate price or terms or anything else for that matter because you still need to sell your house quickly and since you only have one true lead, you need to work with it.

Why? Because you don't have a line of buyers knocking at your door wanting to buy your house.

2.)   You read the book before venturing off to sell your house and you set up this system we have shown you in 20 minutes and you have 50 really interested buyers calling you. The best thing about your strategy is that you get to cherry pick the best buyers that WILL agree to your terms.

Sure, you will talk somethings over with the buyer but overall, you get what you want because you know you have a line of buyers wanting the house and at least one of them will accept your terms and price.

If… and you are in a situation where you need to negotiate, always, have reasons to back up your asking price and/or terms. The key to avoiding negotiations is to have a lot of buyers interested in your house.

And the key to easy negotiations is to have numbers to back you up and staying firm on what you want. If they don't agree, it's ok. You will have another potential buyer waiting that will find your terms, price and house perfect for their family

CHAPTER 10

Schedule Closing With an Attorney

Once your buyer verbally agrees to buy your house, we recommend you contact a real estate attorney to draft the paperwork and close the transaction. What we have found is the scariest part of selling a house is the dreaded paperwork. That's why we recommend you let a professional handle everything for you!

When you meet with an attorney, you and the buyer will sign a Standard Purchase and Sales Agreement and anything else your state requires to close the transaction.

You can reference a Residential Standard Purchase and Sales Agreement on your county website.

Since closing in different states can be different, we recommend you consult your Real Estate Attorney for more details. The Attorney will take you through the process of closing the transaction.

All you will have to do is type into Google, "real estate attorney (your city)" and a few should pop up in the search results. From there, call one and set up an appointment.

CHAPTER 11

Consider A Real Estate Investor

Another great option to consider is talking to a local real estate investor. In every city, there are always real estate investors serving their local community and homeowners in your situation. Investors can pay cash for houses quickly and can offer you a reasonable price.

It is often misunderstood what real estate investors actually do.

Investor's usually work behind the scenes and don't publically announce their good works they do throughout their local communities.

Real Estate Investors are responsible for:

1.) **Raising Property Values**

When a house is vacant in a neighborhood, that will decrease property values for the houses in close proximity to the vacant house. If a house looks worn down and needs major repairs, the same thing happens-reduces property values throughout the neighborhood. Investors buy the vacant houses, repair them and sell them to a new family. This in turn, increase property values throughout the neighborhood.

2.) **Paying Cash For Houses**

Investors are known for paying cash for houses. Since an investor pays cash for houses, they can close quickly because they don't have to wait for a bank loan. This also means, they can buy a house "As-Is" and the house is not subject to an inspection before they purchase. With a bank, they would require an inspection and if the house fails the inspection-the bank will not loan any money.

Investors can take unwanted houses off homeowners backs at any time by giving the homeowner cash.

3.) **They Provide Buying Options For Home Buyers**

Investors help many home buyers whether it's a family looking to buy a house or an individual that has bad credit-get into a house they deserve. You see, since the 2007 stock market crash, many people are facing many challenges including a poor credit score. Due to the banks tightening up lending standards, many people cannot get loans for houses anymore due to poor credit scores. This makes it increasingly hard to sell a house nowadays. In our opinion, just because people have bad credit scores doesn't mean they are bad people. They are just people that need a different financing solution. We believe everyone deserves to live where they truly want to.

With that in mind, investors can give people options to buy houses. What this means is that instead of going through a bank, the investor will finance the house personally to a home buyer. In this case, a buyer with a poor credit score can still get into the house of their dreams and not get held up by banks that won't lend money.

4.) Investors Help New Homebuyers Repair Their Credit Through Their Financing Options.

Since investors can provide different buying options to new home buyers, those buying options such as lease purchasing a house (rent to own) or the investor seller financing a house for a buyer can help them repair their credit by making timely and full payments to the investor. In turn, the investor can help the homebuyer get a loan to cash the investor out of the house in the future.

As you know, Matt and I are real estate investors in the Eau Claire WI and Twin Cities, MN area and we couldn't have picked a more fulfilling career!

Why should you call a real estate investor?

Simply because it gives you another option to sell your house! It is always good to explore your options and we recommend exploring all options. The more options you have on the table the better decision you can make.

Whether your house is vacant, in need of major or minor repair, your house is pretty, investors are very interested in your house!

How can a real estate investor help me?

Investors will evaluate your situation and your property and then come up with a solution based on the information you give them. The offer may be an all cash offer or some other financing offer. Either way, an investor will provide you with a solution that they can offer. Again, these are just options you can consider when selling your house. If you decide to choose one of their options, the purchase and transaction will happen very quickly helping you get on with your life! There is never any pressure and the decision is yours to make! When you talk to an investor, your information is completely confidential.

How does the process work when working with an investor?

First, you will want to research and locate investors in your local area. Look for signs, newspaper ads, look on Google.com and find one that looks professional. Then, give them a call and tell them about your situation and your house. Once you have built your website that tells all the information about your house, simply send them your url to view.

Second, the investor will assess your information and research your house and make you an offer. The offer could be an all cash offer or a different financing option, or both.

Third, you decide to take the offer or not. There's never any pressure to take the offer. It is simply an option you can consider!

Forth, if you choose to take the offer, the investor will schedule a closing with a local attorney that works on your schedule and the purchase will be complete quickly.

It is a very simple process and you have the choice to make your own personal decision that makes sense for your situation and your family!

"If you are in the Eau Claire WI or Twin Cities MN area, you can always give us a call to go over your options. We are excited to talk with you and discuss your situation in a confidential environment!"

844.526.1990

To help you out even further we offer consulting services to help homeowners sell their houses fast on their own. We teach many homeowners step by step how to sell their houses and answer any questions they may have. We help them with the paperwork and we guide them through their marketing journey.

Sometimes, the best thing to do is learn from somebody that has achieve what you want to achieve such as selling your house. We continue to add services to our business because our clients have different needs and situations. We want to continue to live our mission of helping anyone that calls our office or visits our website sell their house!

Final Word

Now, you have what you need to sell your own house!

You now know more than 99% of home sellers using our personal strategies to sell houses in 30 days or less.

Now it's time to take action. It's time for you to start the process and implement what you now know!

The worst thing I can imagine is that you have all this knowledge now and you don't take action.

Without action, you don't get results.

Remember, we are always here to help! And...we want to hear about your success. When you sell your house, tell us! We would love to hear about your success!

Simply email your success stories to info@eauclairehomebuyers.com and we will draw one name each month and send you a special gift worth $100!

Happy Selling! Get at it!

Mitch and Matthew Hell
Eau Claire Home Buyers
http://EauClaireHomeBuyers.com
844.526.1990

30 Day Success Formula Checklist

This checklist outlines the success formula for your reference, so once you have gone through our entire 30 day success formula program, This checklist will help you organize your tasks in one place to make it easy to implement.

And making it easy, is the best way to sell your house quickly!

30 Day Success Formula Checklist

Getting The Price Right

___Have you asked a Realtor for comparable sales data? See scripts in book for reference.

___Have you looked your house up on Zillow or Eapprasial.com to compare it to what the Realtor estimated your houses worth?

___Have you made a list of all the repairs needed or all the enhancements to your house? This is to back up the price you ask for.

___Have you come up with a price? Write it here _____

Get The House Ready To Sell

Bathroom:

___New Shower Curtain
___Towels on hangers
___New toilet paper roll
___Throw rug in front of sink
___Flowers on toilet top

Kitchen:

___Small pant on counter top
___Fill paper towel holder
___Counters are empty and cleaned
___Rug in front of sink
___Sink is cleaned

___Curtains on windows if applicable

Living Room:

___Depersonalize all pictures and walls
___Welcome Rug in doorway
___Plants by doorway
___Fireplace cleaned

Lawn:

___Grass is cut and lawn is clean
___Clutter or garbage is removed
___Garbage cans emptied

Be Ready To Receive Buyer Phone Calls

___Have set up your simple website to save you time and to sell your house faster?
___Have you set up your Flickr account to save you time?

Locate Potential Buyers

Craigslist

___Have you wrote your ad as specified in the book to attract a ton of buyers?
___Have you took good pictures of the front and back of your house?
___Have you posted to Craiglist.com?
___Did you put your website address and Flickr address in your post?
___Have posted it in the correct categories as specified in the book?
___Are you posting your ad every 3 days to stay on top of search results?

Facebook

___Have you found your local "Stuff for sale" group and posted in it?
___Do you have a good following on Facebook? Yes or No
___Have your posted your house on your timeline as specified in the book?
___Did you ask for the like and share?

Yard Signs

___Did you gather all the supplies?
___Did you hand write your signs before putting them out?
___Have you posted them properly in your yard? Like a carnival?
___Have you located high traffic areas in your city/town to place your signs?

___Have you peppered your city/town with your signs-Recommended 30 per week.

Video Tour

___Do you have a camera? A smartphone is a great camera to use
___Have you recorded your tour as specified in the book?
___Have you created your Youtube channel?
___Have you uploaded your video properly as specified in the book to get maximum exposure on Google.com?

Pre-screen Potential Buyers

___Are you asking the 3 questions we mentioned in the book to make sure you are dealing only with buyers that have money to buy your house?
___Have you asked for proof of funds?
___Are you using the 2 step question series to make sure you are getting the most for your house?
___Are you directing your buyers to your website to see all the information so they can make an easy buying decision?

Meet With Buyer And Show Your House

___Have you set aside at least 2 hours to follow up and show your house?
___Have you made an appointment?

Schedule Closing With An Attorney

___Have you Googled a local Real Estate Attorney or Title Company for closing?
___Have you called the Attorney or Title Company to set up closing?
___Have you called Buyer about time and location of closing?
___Have you gathered all information the Attorney or Title Company suggested you bring to closing?

Close The Deal, Sell Your House

___Have you cashed your check and went out to dinner to celebrate your success?

There you have it, a complete checklist-Step By Step to sell your house in 30 days or less.

If you have any questions, please don't hesitate to connect with us!

Mitch and Matthew Hell
EauClaireHomeBuyers.com
FSBO 30 Day Success Formula Book

ABOUT THE AUTHORS

Mitch and Matthew Hell are the masterminds behind "For Sale By Owner 30 Day Success Formula". With over 5 years of helping motivated sellers move their houses and over 10 combined years of marketing experience, the brothers know what does work and what doesn't work in Today's new real estate market. Mitch and Matthew specialize in forming creative real estate solutions to difficult real estate problems. When the brothers are not working real estate deals and helping homeowners, Mitch enjoys physical fitness training, self-defense training, motivational life coaching and traveling. Matthew enjoys trying new restaurants, making the best latte on earth and time with his family!

Eau Claire Home Buyers